Changing Light

Jenny Sofield

© Jenny Sofield

All rights reserved. No part of this publication may be reproduced, stored in a retrieval system, or transmitted in any form or by any means, electronic, mechanical, photocopying, recording or otherwise, without the prior written permission of the author.

National Library of Australia Cataloguing-in-Publication entry

Author: Sofield, Jenny, author.

Title: Changing Light / Jenny Sofield.

ISBN: 9780992372804 (paperback)

Subjects: Poetry.

Dewey Number: A821.4

Published with the assistance of www.loveofbooks.com.au

'This first (and hopefully not last!) anthology expresses delicately and honestly some of the unbearable griefs and losses of life: of ALL our lives, except that few of us have the courage needed to expose that grief openly, movingly, and work on it in the most positive of ways: creation, "Moving On" out of unhappiness. Jennifer has done just that in the writing of these poems, a collection that everyone can connect with.'

Diana Ettinger

'It is a real pleasure to see this second volume of poems from Jennifer, a very exciting up and coming award winning poet. There is a real understanding and empathy in her writing that many people will be able to relate to.'

Noeleen Kuss

'Jenny's poems manage to capture the feelings we have about so many of the experiences in our lives. Sometimes they are the small, almost ordinary moments that without capturing them, would slip by, unremarked, unremembered. It is those moments that we don't take the time to examine but ultimately help make us who we are. Her poems made me catch my breath at some of the emotions that I felt when reading, giving greater meaning to similar experiences in my own life. This is a touching and poignant search for self.'

Julia Monhaghan.

Acknowledgements

So many people have helped in the writing of these poems. I am very grateful to everyone who contributed in some way, and especially to:

My family:
> My sister for far too much to list here!
> My mother (Mummy - and for being much braver than she realises)
> My Father, for being willing to read these poems along the way.

Diana for being my 'oldest' friend and knowing me better than anyone and judging me the least!

Georgie: for believing I could write.
Ann: for our ongoing friendship and your continual support.
Patrick: I am not sure you know how much I appreciate your patience from all those years ago
Edward, Jenny and Sam – I love you.
Noeleen: for the BS (fun) review!!

I would also like to add for this second volume, absent friends:
> Sarah Raphael. You will always be in my memories.
> And Nicholas for literally saving my life when my coat caught on fire.

And finally anyone I have not mentioned and whom I may have missed out!

Dedication

To Paul
Thank You

Contents

Waiting	11
Nothing Cure	12
Unimportant	13
Lies	17
Compliments Are Such Sweet Sorrow	18
No Prizes	19
A Rare Woman	17
Yearning	18
In The Car	19
IVF	20
Despair	21
What Was It?	22
Someone Else's Child	23
Flowers	24
Hell	25
Whatever I Feel	26
Ironic Friendship	27
Cried Out	28
Leaving	29
Grief	30
Exposure	31
Old Love	32
Flags	33
Final Love	34
Alien Nation	36
Dislocation	37
Hangover	38
Legacy	39
Dead Dreams	40
In Defence OF Memories	41
Healing	42

Not Ready	43
Real Meaning	44
Alcohol	45
Fear	46
Painkiller	47
Dusk	48
Unfinished Business	49
Inner Child	50
Amour Fou	51
Depression	52
Friendship	57
Turning 21	56
Missing	58
Love And War	59

WAITING

Overwhelming
Cloud confusion
Sound...distorted
Touch...unyielding
Sight...sightless
Walking
Talking
I'm here
Breathing,
Alive,
But not living.

And there you are
Knowing
Listening
Following
But never encroaching
Watching
Waiting
But never demanding.

And then the
Cloud confusion breaks
Easing
Soothing
Mist diffusing
Time forgiving
Now I'm here
Breathing
Living.

And there you are
Always there.

NOTHING CURE

Emptiness
Veils my spirit.
Reach inside;
Nothing.
Depression;
Nothing.
No feelings
And yet
I want to run,
Hide,
Disobey –
But for what?
To numb.
The numbness.

Emptiness.
I watched you cry;
Nothing.
I heard your tenderness;
Nothing.
Reach inside
Dead living
Living dead
No wake
No good byes
Nothing.
Run.
Hide.
To numb.
The numbness.

UNIMPORTANT

I needed you
I wanted you
To say
'I missed you too'
And be
As pleased
To see me.

I needed you
Or was the
Void
Reflected
From a different
Time
And place.
It's not your fault
The ache
Inside
Was mine.

But I'm
Still hurt
You barely
Said hello.

LIES

Tell me again
How she loved me,
Tell me again
How it showed,
Actions rarely tell lies
For once
I believe you
She can't look me
Straight in the eyes.

And you
How did you love me
Love her,
Tell me once more
How it showed.
Actions speak louder
Than words,
I believe you
You said her suspicions
Were lies
But she saw the truth
In your eyes.

Tell me at all
That you love me,
Tell me at all
That it shows,
I hugged her
She stood like a stone,
Her actions spoke volumes
No Lies.
God how you both must
Love me,
You can't face the look
In my eyes.

COMPLIMENTS ARE SUCH SWEET SORROW

You said
The loveliest
Words,
You said them
About me.
It feels unreal
Surreal,
They belong
To a different
Person
Time
And place.

You said
The loveliest
Words,
Touching,
Moving,
Strangely
Sad.
The things you
Said
About me
Were only dreams,
Unreal,
Surreal,
They found me
Remembering
A different time
And place.

NO PRIZES

You taught me many things,
Passion,
Love,
And through the hue
Of child eyes
I looked at you
And idolised.
I look back
Fondly,
Memories
Are soft.
This place,
Hot and dusty – but at night
Purple seeps
Through fuchsia red,
Sweet smell
Of drug filled skies.
I looked at you
And Idolised.

You taught me many things,
That you are
Beautiful.
Passion
Comes in many guises,
Fight for
Love,
Fight for everything
You want,
Life hurts,
Adulthood is full
Of pain,
Love hurts.
There are no prizes
For the child who idolises.

A RARE WOMAN

My mother
Says it isn't great.
My mother says
Life has more
To offer.
She is sad,
Lonely.
She'll call me.
She'll cry.

My mother
Says
There are many
Other things
To keep me
Occupied.
She tells it as it is.
She doesn't lie.

My mother
Says it isn't great.
She turns
To me,
Her child.
In and out
Of sobbing
Says,
I need to know
My children love me
Or I'll die.

YEARNING

She is older,
She is wiser
So I ask
"This yearning for a child,
does it ever go away?"
She looks at me,
Eyes shimmering
With Pain
And says
"Life will never be the same."

She is older,
She is wiser,
So I tell her how I feel
And her blue eyes
Pierce me with
Their pain.
I want to kiss her
Because I know
I have reminded her again.

She is older,
She is wiser,
So I say nothing.
Her glance
Tells me of her pain.
We just
Hold the moment
And listen to the rain.

IN THE CAR

I am sitting
In the car.
Music,
Sunshine,
A whole world
Out there.

But inside
These four doors
I'm in
A different place.
Tears trickle,
At first
Slow motion
From the corners
Of my eyes.

And then
A stream
Runs down my neck.
I do not want
To wipe it dry,
Wipe this acknowledgment
Away.

I cannot move.
I feel
A thousand years
Of sadness
In a single surge
And I wear
My sunglasses
To hide my swollen eyes.
I do not want
To dry my face,
Wipe this acknowledgment
Away.

IVF

All the while
I was trying
It connected me
To hope,
Like the woman
Who miscarried
And said
The pain was pleasure.
Once gone
Everything was gone.

All the while
I was trying
I was hopeful.
The waiting time
Had promise.
Like the woman said
The pain had life.
When it was gone
The embryos were gone.
Everything was gone.

DESPAIR

Click clack
Train track,
Crashing rain
Lines across
The window pane.
World out there
Cold and bare.
I've left you
Feeling such despair.

Good grief,
Disbelief,
Thick clouds
Dreams in shrouds,
Mourning.
What has not been fair.
I didn't want to leave you
Feeling such despair.

WHAT WAS IT?

Rain dripping
Warm streams
Down the window pane.
Sunday afternoon
Has spun around again.
Pixels flickering.
Boring images.
Longing for the weekend,
Longing for something
To do.
I miss those times
Doing whatever it was
With you.

Rain unceasing
In its dreary pace.
Dull T. V.
And we just sit
And stare
As if we're barely there.
Have we forgotten
How to be together…
Waiting for the weekend,
Waiting for something to do
To remind me
Of whatever it was
I used to do with you.

SOMEONE ELSE'S CHILD

She says
"When you hold
Someone else's child
It's not the same.
Your feelings
Cannot be the same.
It's not your child."
And then she speaks again.
Is she unsure,
I do not understand,
Is this what makes her
Repeat
'It's not your child.
It's not your child.'

I do not anticipate
This seizure,
This violence
Of feeling.
With respect
She cannot understand
This pain, this agony
When life
Again
Unexpectedly reminds me
It's not my child.
It can never be my child.

FLOWERS

Flowers
To say I'm sorry,
Flowers
To show regret,
Flowers
To ease my guilt,
Flowers
After a fight.
Is she right?
Is anger
All they really say?

Flowers
To say I love you,
Flowers
To say I miss you,
Flowers
On a birthday.
What message
Did I really send?
And is she right,
Is anger
All that flowers say?

HELL

I am in hell
And you know it,
Blame myself
And you do nothing
To change my mind.
You just walk by
And smile,
A cycle of
Teasing
And hurting.
I try to speak.
I am confused
As you do not
Turn to look at me.

I am in hell
Spiralling
Downwards,
Just sit and stare
And want to bang
My head.
I hope this isn't
The time
I leave a note saying
"I'm dead."

WHATEVER I FEEL

I am not sure
What I feel.
I know I feel.
Memories have stirred
A hornets' nest.
I am calm.
I am learning
If it hurts
It's real,
Whatever it is
I feel.

I am sad,
Scared.
When I coldly
Plan my death
I see your face,
See you crying.
I stop these
Plans for dying.
I am learning
I Need to feel.
My fear of suicide
Is real.

IRONIC FRIENDSHIP

It is so ironic.
Weakness,
Failings,
You always defended,
Persuaded me
Not to judge
Or belittle
But lift,
Always lift spirit.
Yet you broke mine.

It is so ironic.
We share
A common past,
A duplicity of pain
Which makes it
Really sad
That you closed
The door today.
Always lift spirit.
Except for mine.

CRIED OUT

Sometimes
I think
I have cried enough
To last a lifetime.
And then
Feelings
From my past
Remind me
Of the force
With which
A human heart
Can grieve and weep.

When calm
I hope
I'll never feel again
This depth of sadness,
This devastation.
I thought
I was over
All the pain.
But I woke.
And I had
Been crying
In my sleep.

LEAVING

After you went
Everything felt heavy,
The room
Felt twice as big,
And waiting...
Empty waiting...
Felt unbearable.
I did not want
To go
Or stay alone.

After I left
The journey
I have done
So many times
Felt twice as long,
Tears paralleled
The rain,
And every extra pain
Felt one too many.

Home now.
Waiting...
Waiting...
By the phone.
It was so difficult,
Travelling alone.

GRIEF

They say it's
Just a passing phase,
You're sad.
A bit of grief.

So I sit and wait
Lie awake
But still
There's no relief.

Insomnia.
I like the night.
This world
I feel so awful in
Goes quiet.

But then,
I have the time
To think and analyse
And sometimes
It's four am
Before I close my eyes.

They say
I will recover.
I won't always feel
This sad.

But I'm not sure
What I believe.
So I sit and wait
And slowly start to grieve.

EXPOSURE

It is the deepest place
I know,
The most fragile part
Of every human being,
The blue print of a soul.
And she touched it.
She did not put the weakness
There,
She did not break my heart.
But she reached in uninvited
And I wish I could have
Stemmed the flow.

This is the place
That binds my world together.
Here
Everything I think and feel
Is etched upon my soul.
And she touched this part of me.
She did not crush my feelings.
She did not wreck my heart.
But I was unprepared.
And I wish I'd never shown
Such raw distress.

Winner of the 2002 'Bedfordshire Prize' in February 2002.
The Bedford Open Poetry Competition, England
Published in 'The Interpreter's House'.

OLD LOVE

You haunt my
Mind,
My soul,
And I dream
Of you.
Memories
Tell a thousand stories.
The sun sets
Over the horizon
But it never dies.
Love sets
In time
But it never
Lies.

FLAGS

Flags
Tell me
Which way the wind
Is blowing,
How hard
The gusts chatter
And memories
Flutter
In my mind.
Every now and then
The flags
Change direction
And I know
You are still
With me.
My windsock
Tells me
There was a
Kind of loving,
Harsh at times,
But always full of life.

FINAL LOVE

It wasn't
Just
Grown men
Crying,
Friends
Choking as they
Tried to piece
Together
The story
Of his life;
It wasn't
Just
Hundreds of people
Sitting in every place
On every pew
And more
Standing at the back.

It wasn't
Just
The palpable
Support
Of one to another
As the grief
Became too much,
Nor the four
Tiny circles
Flecked
At the edges
After the tears
Had landed
On the terracotta tiles.

It was
The weight
That hung in the air.
This was the measure
Of love.

ALIEN NATION

Sometimes
I wonder
What is wrong
With the world.
No one sees
As I see.
No one thinks
As I think.
Am I an alien,
Completely out of place?

What is wrong
With the world,
Socially constrained
By must do,
Ought to do,
Have to do.
Am I paranoid
When I think
Everybody else
Is watching me?
Delusional
When I think
I'm the only one
Who understands?

What is wrong
Or who is wrong,
And which one of us
Is completely
Off the planet,
Somewhere out of space?

DISLOCATION

A room
Full of friends
At a funeral
Becomes a room
Full of names,
Collective sorrow
Weeping separately,
Each pair of eyes
Looking
In their own direction,
Each tear
Starting from
A different place
That joins
This sadness
With their past
And all I can do
Is stare and watch
As if I have no past.
A man's voice,
The first note,
The sharp
Intake of breath
As the coffin
Is lifted
Unites this grief.

But faces
Still look unfamiliar,
And I don't know
What I feel.

HANGOVER

Partial memory,
Chunks of time
Lost,
Shocked,
Embarrassed,
Anxious,
I might have
Hurt you
When I let
My drunken soul
Lie bare.

Enjoyed the comfort,
Touch,
Softness,
Of your body
Close to mine.

Now that I am sober,
I hope you will
Forgive
This dropping of
My guard,
This exposure
Now you've seen
My drunken soul
Lie bare.

LEGACY

There are days
When gaps
I have bridged
Reopen,
Where I end up
Wrestling
A self of old,
Moments
When I forget
I have reconciled
Life's failings,
Feel angry
With this legacy
Of need
And my inability
To let it go.
On days like this
I wish I could morph
Into a different person.

DEAD DREAMS

What shall I wear
To the funeral?
Black to mourn
The passing
Of all hope
Or colours
To celebrate
The end of the
Struggle?
Will I reflect
And say a eulogy
Or regret
All those
Wasted hours?
This is a wake
For one.
This is the death
Of child illusions,
Dreams cremated.
How will I say good-bye
And where shall I
Spread the ashes?

IN DEFENCE OF MEMORIES

Please don't say
My memories
Are illusions,
Children Exaggerate
And colour the truth.

Please don't explain
Growing up
Is a fairground mirror,
Reflections
Distorted

Please don't tell me
Children
Are half blind.
They do see differently
But adults
judge the view.

HEALING

It feels
Like an old friend,
Warm and
Familiar,
Something
From a past
I thought
I'd left behind.
It feels
Like a place
I know well,
Rooms I can name.
I am walking
In heavy boots
And for a moment
I cannot breathe,
But there is
Comfort
In this weight,
This lack of air.
It tells me
I have moved on.

NOT READY

I came to you
Needing to
Say the same things
Over and over…
And wanted you
To listen,
Even if
The truth is
I have to change.

I came to you
Looking
For a place
To hide,
Just for a
Little longer…
The truth is
You are not
The right person
To take cover with
And I am
Not ready for reality
When I am with you.

REAL MEANING

I wasn't asking
For advice,
If you
Thought
I had a problem.
I wasn't asking
If you knew
How I might feel –
I was asking you
To listen
Between the lines.

I didn't need
Your help.
I was trying to tell you
I have done
Some crazy things.
No excuses.
I know I have
A problem.
I just wanted you
To hear
Between the lines.

ALCOHOL

Alcohol.
It feels like,
A gentle
Aphrodisiac,
A subtle persuader,
A potent mix
That gives me courage,
Lifting,
Drowning,
A powerful elixir,
Gradually changing
The view.

Hangover.
A blinding headache,
Paranoid cocktail,
Spaced out disappointment,
My brain
Soaked
Dragging me
Into a familiar,
dark place.

Alcohol.
Hypnotic, persuasive,
A liquid line
That blurs the edges
Of ecstasy
And pain,
A powerful elixir
And I am not sure
Where I am
In the haze.

FEAR

It is
Not the feelings
But the intensity,
Waves
Crashing through
My soul.
It is
The avalanche
Of living,
Pushing at the
Paradigm of life,
The intrusion
Of my heart
Into my comfortable
World.
This is what scares me.

It is not the height
When I climb
Nor the drop
When I look down.
I have no fear.
But when I fall
I am afraid
Of where I'll land.

PAINKILLER

Head is full
Of crazy thoughts,
Half lobotomised
With drink,
I'm staring
At a box of pills
And I don't know
What to think.
I move the tablets,
Pick them up
And wonder what to do.
I know
You'll find me
If I swallow just a few,
Not enough to die
But to send
Me off to sleep.
I am hurting
And have long forgotten
How to weep.
I know I'm acting
Senseless,
This plan is quite insane
But it isn't some
Mad death wish.
I just want to
Kill the pain.

DUSK

Sunrise,
Sunset.
One softly
Easing into dawn
Washing over everything
With all the promise
Of the day,
The other
Melting,
Fading
Taking with it
Memories,
Knowledge
That nothing
Stays.
I cannot hold this moment
Slipping
Through my grasp,
I cannot hold you.

Sunrise,
Sunset,
Dusk has fallen
And I do not want
To say
Goodbye.

UNFINISHED BUSINESS?

I wish she was alive
I wish she wasn't dead
I wish I could take back
The things I did and said

I wish she could have known
It wasn't really me
That I really loved her
In my hurt and jealousy

I wish that in my childhood
I'd been a little kinder
And in my adulthood
I wish I'd tried to find her

I wish I'd had the chance
To say sorry for the pain,
That she could see me now
And we could start again.

I wish she was alive
And not just in my tears.
She is such a part of me,
Of my tender growing years.

INNER CHILD

A path,
A forest
Sand
And sea,
And someone
Waits for me.

They are older,
Wiser,
And as the
Water
Licks the sand,
They take my
tiny hand.

I am small
And they are
Tall.
We walk
But do not talk
And then
I retrace
My steps -
Sand,
Forest,
Back along
The path.
And I know
With the gentle
Rolling of the sea
Someone,
Older,
Wiser
Always waits for me.

ARMOUR FOU

I wish
I'd kept my diaries,
Ramblings
Of a time
When life was
Honest,
Passionate,
Dangerous perhaps;
When love was everything
And life without
Was nothing.

I wish
I'd kept my journals,
Heartfelt,
Sad,
A time
When life
Hurt with
Every breath
But not to
Breathe with you
Was death.

I wish
I'd kept
Those pages,
Now just memories
Tucked away
And which
So rarely
see
The light of day.

DEPRESSION

At its darkest
I feel
The weight
Of the world
Bearing down
And time
Pins the day
To the ground.
Each step,
If any,
Takes a monumental
Effort
And my tears
Barely
Make a sound.

But I do know
Light,
How it is
To feel
Propelled by hope,
To love,
To laugh
And let life
Carry me.
I do know
Happiness
And joy
And what it is
To simply be.

At its darkest
I feel so heavy.
It's hard
To remember
That even
On the blackest
Night,
The Earth
Is moving
Slowly
Into light.

FRIENDSHIP

Friendship.

What makes
A friendship?
Honesty,
Loyalty,
Birthday cards
Every year,
Not speaking up
Out of fear?

Friendships.

Rhythmic
As they to and fro
But can they
Morph
As people change
And grow?
Time
Slowly peeled
The layers away
And I tried to
Stay,
Juggling our differences,
Loving you
But
Slowly,
Slowly,
Not knowing
What to do.

Friendship.

Sometimes
Love
In the end
Is not enough.
It isn't that
I'm not your friend,
You just couldn't hear
When I spoke up
Without the fear.

TURNING 21

My friend's eldest
Is turning twenty one.
She gets to be
A little jealous
Of her daughter
And buy a tuxedo
For her son.

We fertilised!
Lonely,
Silent
Splitting cells
Waiting for the chance
To grow and nourish.
I had hoped
I'd be the one
To help you flourish
And you might
Have been my daughter
Turning twenty one,
Or I'd be buying
A tuxedo
For my son.

I still think
About what might
Have been
Who you would
Have looked liked.
I miss you
Nearly every day
My silent
Splitting cells,
Dividing
In a petri dish

Trying to
Fulfil
My aching wish.
I would have liked
The chance
To be a little Jealous of
My daughter
Turning twenty one
And to buy
A tuxedo
For my son.

MISSING

We were all
A little grey
Around the edges,
Faces
Half familiar
And knowing laughs
As we crowded
Round
The photographs.

Images
Black and white,
Dated clothes,
Scruffy hair,
I know it was
Impossible
To have you there.
I missed you
In the throng
Of laughs
As we time travelled
Through
The photographs.

We were
All a little grey,
Reminiscing,
Catching up,
The group
Somehow incomplete.
Absent laughs
As I stood
Staring
At the photographs.

LOVE AND WAR

I met you
In my conflict years
When love was war
And being angry
Meant I loved you more.

I met you
When life
Was struggling to survive
And fighting meant
At least I was alive.

I met you
When I hardly knew
Myself,
When love was pain
And I hurt you time and
Time again.

I met you
In my conflict years
When love and envy
Raged inside,
And I felt so small
Standing by your side.

www.ingramcontent.com/pod-product-compliance
Lightning Source LLC
Chambersburg PA
CBHW051710090426
42736CB00013B/2638